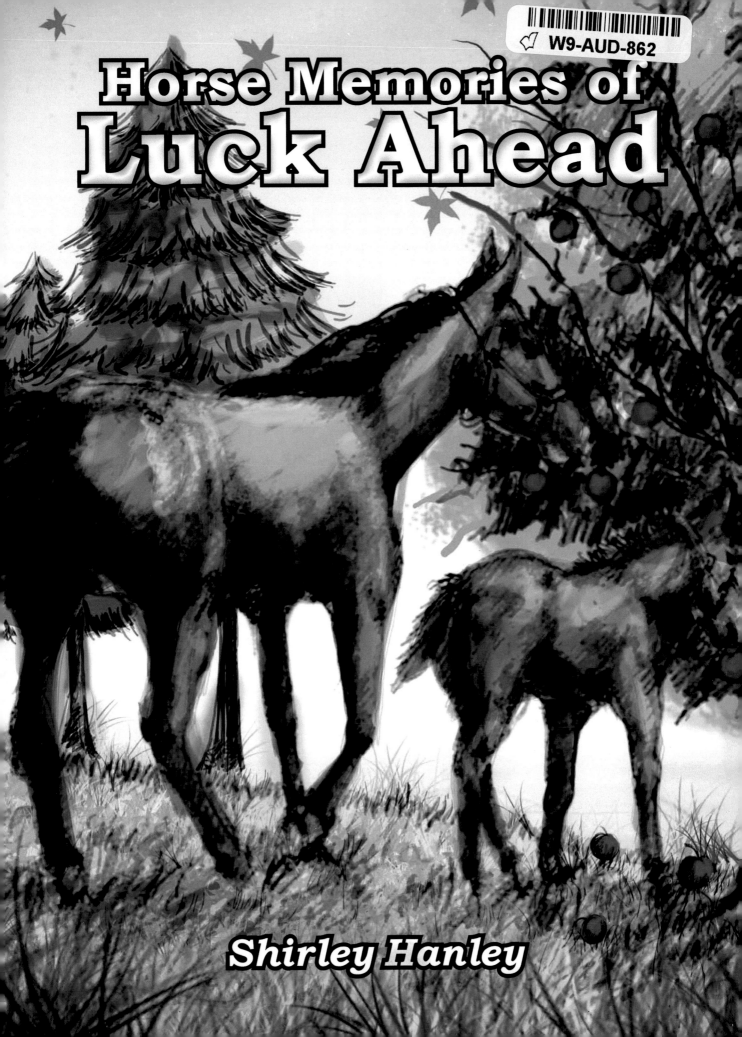

Horse Memories of
Luck Ahead

Shirley Hanley

Copyright © 2010 by Shirley Hanley. 69550-HANL
Library of Congress Control Number: 2010902880
ISBN: Softcover   978-1-4500-5429-4
           Hardcover   978-1-4500-5430-0

This book was printed in the United States of America.

To order additional copies of this book, contact:
Xlibris Corporation
1-888-795-4274
www.Xlibris.com
Orders@Xlibris.com

Horse Memories of Luck Ahead

Shirley Hanley

Luck Ahead was an old race horse. She loved to lean against the barn on

Grampy O'Hanley's farm and just let the sun soak into her tired old body.

Luck Ahead was very old. She knew she didn't have many years left to share with her fillies and colts. She wasn't afraid to leave them, she would be glad to finally rest. She did worry, however, about how her fillies and colts would feel after she was gone. As she watched her offspring racing back and forth in the pasture she remembered when she had spent her days doing the same thing.

One night after coming into her stall with its fresh bed of straw and eating her grain and hay, *Luck Ahead* lay down, content and happy to finally call it a day.

She started dreaming of running in a race like she use to in her younger days. She saw a wonderful bright light appear ahead on the track. The bright light reminded her of racing toward the finish line. She was ahead of all the other horses and knew that she was going to reach the finish line first.

She ran faster and faster toward the bright light until she felt like she was flying. She felt young and free.

The next morning when Grampy O'Hanley came to feed *Luck Ahead* he found her lying in her stall, she had died.

Luck's Lazy Lady and *Miss Annie K* and all the other colts and fillies were playing in the pasture waiting for their mother to come and join them like she did everyday. Even though *Luck Ahead* liked to just lean against the barn in the sun, the young horses liked to see her standing there. They loved to come up and nuzzle her; to feel her soft nose kissing them or to hide under her tail, keeping the flies off their face.

She didn't come out and she didn't come out. They waited one day; two days; three days. *Luck's Lazy Lady* finally realized that her mother would never come out to join them again.

Allusive Miss Eden, the first and oldest of *Luck Ahead's* fillies, told the other horses their mother had died and not to be sad. " Mother was old and tired and ready to rest forever."

She told her brothers and sisters to remember all the happy times they had had with their mother. "Remember all the things she taught you? Like how a race horse should always have a big heart."

Allusive Miss Eden said, "Remember how she always said that a horse should always try to win a race. How horses should always be gentle and loving around children.

As fall was coming and the leaves were turning, the *Lady* remembered how her
mother had taught her to eat the apples off the low hanging branches of the apple
trees. After eating grass all day This was like dessert.

Allusive Miss Eden said, "Remember how she told us never to be afraid of trying something different." She told them how Grampy O'Hanley had given her pink peppermints one day after she had won a race. She crunched them between her teeth and it made her mouth feel like fresh air.

14

Lucks's Lazy Lady told her brothers and sisters about one of the best races their
mother had ever won. It was on a beautiful winter night, the snow was lightly
falling and the lights of the race track shone brightly down on all the horses.
It was one of the fastest races of her lifetime.

Another winter night near Christmas time Grampy O'Hanley hung bells around her neck, dressed up like Santa Clause, and paraded around and around the racetrack. Christmas music was being played over the loud speaker and everyone was singing and wishing each other Merry Christmas.

Remembering their mother telling them about winning a race on St. Patrick's Day made them all feel happy. She told them that everyone was wearing green. The race programs were green, the concession stands sold green beer and green ice cream. She wore green bandages on her legs and a furry green nose guard on her head. The driver wore a green and white outfit. When she won the race she was awarded a green blanket that said "St. Patrick's Day 1971."

As the days and the weeks went by, it helped to remember these happy times. *Luck's Lazy Lady* told the horses how her mother had taught her to race with the cars. As the cars drove along the country road, *Lady* would race along beside them in the pasture. She was so happy when she could beat the cars to the corner of the paddock. She was learning how to be a race horse just like her mother.

When summer came, they all remembered this was the time the new babies would be born. They had to show them how to run like a race horse with their feet flying, their tails blazing behind and heads up high.

As the years and the seasons passed by, *Luck Ahead's* children realized they had wonderful memories to pass on to their own children.

As they ran in the beautiful green pasture they looked up at the sky. A ray of sunlight was beaming down on Grampy O'Hanley's barn right where their mother had loved to stand. It made her children feel that she was still watching over them. "We love you mother."